ORIENTAL

BELLY DANCE

KEMAL ÖZDEMİR

ISBN 975-7054-11-9

Text:
Kemal Özdemir

Translation:
Dr. Dara Çolakoğlu

Layout:
Dönence Basım ve Yayın Hizmetleri

Cover:
Fatih M. Durmuş

Dancer on the Front Cover:
Prenses Banu

Typesetting:
AS&64 Ltd. Şti.
(Hakan Alan)

Photography:
Güngör Özsoy, Mustafa Şapçı,
Tahsin Aydoğmuş, Haluk Özözlü
Dönence Diabank Archives.

Printed in Turkey by
Asır Matbaacılık Ltd. Şti.

Published by
Dönence Basım ve Yayın Hizmetleri
Çatalçeşme Sokak No.15/2, 34410
Cağaloğlu-İSTANBUL/TURKEY
Tel.: (90.212) 511 18 89   Fax: (90.212) 511 58 83

İstanbul, March 2000

ORIENTAL

BELLY DANCE

KEMAL ÖZDEMİR

DÖNENCE

TABLE OF CONTENTS

FOREWORD

"God spoke the order, ' Be' wi the language of power when he wanted to make himself known and create the universe. A ' godly tune' came to existence. That melody decided on twelve notes. Four dances were born of those twelve notes. One of them is 'çerh' (revolving, circular, pertaining to a wheel, pertaining to the spheres, celestial), the other one is 'raks' (dance), another is 'Mu'allak' (hanging, suspended, uncertain) and ' pertav' (leap, jump, a bowshot) is the fourth...

When God created the universe, he shined his holy light down on it. The whole universe laughed with the pleasure of that light. Four dances which come to be from four instruments and words of twelve notes joined this world.

The four elements complied with those four dances. When water ran, the wheel turned; fire came and joined the dance; when the wind came, the suspended thing turned; and the earth came to become a shot.

Then, God created man and made the whole universe present in man's body. God stamped the universe with wisdom and granted it to man and gave us eyes for us to see it, He gave us ears to hear, a tongue to speak, hands to hold, feet to walk, a heart to know, intellect to understand, a soul to enjoy life, skin for movement and a life for peace. The measure of life is a year. The year has four parts. Spring has three months, summer has three months, fall has three months and winter has three months.

The twelve notes are the twelve months. Four parts conform to four dances. Dead places enliven when spring comes, dried trees get dreesed in green, grass grows on feeble trunks, milk runs through dried veins. The crushing force turns to kindness, the cold to heat and the waste turns to benefit. This is the symbol of "çerh".

When summer comes, the world is at dance. The leaves, flowers and fruits dance. This movement is the symbol of "raks".

Fruits cease to be and leaves turn yellow when fall comes; this is the symbol of suspension and motionlessness. When winter arrives, the shine of the universe vanishes, wet trees dry up and this is the sign of being thrown away, of extinction.

All of these various dances and movements are made of the "godly tune" which comes to existence with the order of " kün" (Be!)[1]

Aşıkpaşa, The Booklet of Dance, 15th century, Ottoman manuscript.

INTRODUCTION

Life is a dance. Rivalry, fights and peace are forms of dance. Dance is the ceremony of breathing, eating, drinking and loving. We were all born to a dancing world.

Dance has been accepted throughout the world as the most ancient form of art. Primitive man used dance or body movements to express what he felt in his feeble struggle against nature. He also expressed his feelings of joy with dance whenever he hunted and fed himself, killed a dangerous wild animal, courted a candidate mate, and even when he succeeded in sexual intercourse and wished to propagate his manliness. He tried to convey his desires and his pain via dance.

Primitive religions acknowledged dance as a part of their rituals since dance triggered man's empathy. We know that the worshipping ritual of primitive religions consisted of a short prayer and then mostly of dance routines.

Dance as a part of religious ceremonies seems not to have satisfied basic human needs. Man continued to dance also in his moments of happiness. In almost all societies, this practice was interpreted as a need for man to express feelings of joy, either as a part of a religious ceremony or as an integral part of daily life. People satisfied their feelings of joy, enthusiasm, relaxation and satisfaction as they danced. Was it not only natural for them to satisfy these feelings in forms other than religious rituals?

Polytheist religions emphasized the role of dance since the beginning of recorded time. In fact, dance was once even regarded as a philosophy of life.

In describing the most proper way of living in his work called "*Laws*," Plato wrote the following, "*Man should live as if he danced; he should play games, sing and dance. By doing so, he will appeal to the Gods and defend himself against his enemies. Thusly, he can win contests.*" Dance is characterized by melody,

Sacred dancers, Egypt, fresco from the 14th century B.C.

playfulness and enthusiasm. Plato's consideration and philosophy of life cited above comprises these three attributes which all dances possess.

Monotheist religions did not condone dance in the beginning in the belief that passionate feelings that dance evoked could not be subdued and controlled. Another reason for this attitude was

Oriental dance in antiquity.

the goal of making believers forget their old beliefs which were identified with dancing ceremonies. But even still, such monotheist religions could not eradicate dance which was a part of human life. Some sects of monotheist religions adopted dance as the method of worship. The Mevlevi sect in Turkey is the best example of this development.

Dance in antiquity.

Dance has been luring man into its magical and irresistible world for centuries. Dance in a social world that was developing and full of complicated relations had gone astray of its function in the days of antiquity, it had become completely civilized.

From the standpoint of exuburance and choreography, there were major differences between the dances that came into existence through the peasantry's struggle against nature and the ballroom dancing of the bourgeois. Different lifestyles in society continued to give rise to new dances. However, we can still say that some special dances stem completely from basic human characteristics. As we can all guess quite easily, these characteristics are clearly defined in dance routines which are full of sensuality.

Considered to be the gateway to the East, Turkey offers a lot of features which nuture oriental dreams. Oriental belly dancing,

Egyptian dancer. 19th century.

long a symbol of the East, has always symbolized the magical attraction of Eastern women and aroused interest in the Western world. Though the travelogues of Western orientalists, which revealed much on the erotic women of the east, were usually sprinkled with highly imaginative power, such written material as well as the engravings by western artists who accompanied the writers kindled this interest immensely during the 17th and 18th centuries. The translation of Eastern literature such as "1001 Arabian Nights," into western languages, and even the Old and New Testament aided in getting people caught up in the spell of oriental dance. Salome, who danced the "Seven Tulles" dance to commemorate John the Baptist, became a symbol of this art. Besides the limited number of written works of the wandering orientalists, some Eastern countries set up pavilions at world exhibitions organized in principal Western

Salome, the symbol of oriental dance.

cities during the 19th century, and hired belly dancers to display their talents there. Those dancers dressed in colorful authentic attire performed their spellbinding dances before curious audiences. Westerners began to enjoy oriental dancers on their own soil from the mid-19th century onwards, whereas they became a part of the western world of entertainment at the beginning of the 20th century. Turkish belly dancers took their traditional dance out to the wider world and enchanted their audiences when they appeared on dance stages in various countries from America to Argentina, from the Arabian

Peninsula to England, and from Japan to Italy. Thus, they removed the rust that had accumulated on the eyes of those who came to watch their shows, mystifying their hearts in the process.

The aim of this book is to introduce Oriental Dance or the Turkish Belly Dance to the reader since it continues to maintain high levels of popularity in the Turkish public. We believe that it will also give you great pleasure as you learn something about the colorful past of the Turkish belly dancing lore.

Oriental belly dancing is the most excellent and most effective aphrodisiac mankind has ever discovered. We hope this book will take you on a dazzling journey through this very special world.

Wishing you a delightfully good time...

Princess Banu.

Asena, the prominent young star on Turkish stages.

THE TURKS AND DANCE

   Central Asia is the original motherland of the Turks who
have a long history and have travelled a long way. Turks lived a
tribal and nomadic life in Central Asia. These tribes, which lived
   under very tough climactic conditions, were famous for their
ability to wage war and they owed their existence to it. They had
a developed culture despite their nomadic way of life. Called "a
civilization of the steppes," theirs is one that has only partly
discovered through archaeological excavations, most of the
revealed treasures of which are displayed at the Hermitage
Museum in St. Petersburg, Russia today. The Turks, who led a
nomadic life intertwined with nature, possessed a shamanistic
belief. The Shaman, who instructed the ritual and acted as
liaision between the people and a god in the heavens, performed

Dancing shamans. Mehmet Siyahkalem (Blackpen), 15th century.

Dancer in the harem.

ceremonial dances to the accompaniment of a tambourine. The Shaman's mythical dance was a part of his journey up to the heavens. We know that the Shaman danced alone during this ritual, and that those watching the ceremony did not participate much in the rituals. The Turks liked to perform to instrumental music at banquets which followed victory battles and happy weddings. In observing the Turks during his journey east in 596

Dancer in the harem.

A.D., the Byzantine traveler, Zemark described a purification ceremony where they danced and spun energetically around a bonfire. It is also known that dance had an important impact in the ritual of hunting, whereas it was customary to dance both before and during the hunt. The most typical dance consisted of men and women forming a circle together, and performing fancy footwork from right to left. Some of dances, which date back

Dancer in the harem.

1,500-2,000 years, are still performed in Anatolia today.

    After they emigrated from Central Asia, the Turks first settled in Iran, ruling these lands as Seljuk Turks, then later on moved on to Anatolia, which has been their homeland for almost 1,000 years,. They had previously adopted the Islam as their religion, but they did not abandon their former traditions. They had peaceful relations with the Islamic Empire and they gradually

Oriental dancer.

took on some elements of Islamic culture they got to know in Iran.

The Turks encountered oriental dance in these lands, whereas it wasn't long before this type of dance, which was not a part of their traditions, won them over with its spell. Chronicles tell us that oriental dancers had participated in the festivities held in Seljuk Palaces and elsewhere.

Carrying with them the influences of Central Asian, Persian and Islamic civilizations, the Turks settled in Anatolia, which was culturally molded by the Byzantine Empire, the heirs of the Roman Empire as well as tens of local civilizations. This rich cultural makeup facilitated the formation of a very colorful atmosphere. The Anatolian peninsula is a piece of land where dance played a wide role in the daily life and religious beliefs of its people. The seasons also dance in sequentially in this geographic region where nature has been very generous.

Oriental dancers at the palace.

The Turks continued down their historical path with the dominance of the Seljuks and the birth of the Ottoman State. The Ottomans extended their empire into Anatolia and the Balkans, ruling over a vast territory, and their world city was Istanbul which had become the capital after the conquest in 1453. Istanbul used to be the place where the sultan and the rich lived. So, it was not unusual, for the performance arts to develop in the capital and to be cherished by its population. Istanbul was the place where oriental dance, which was also akin to the Byzantine heritage, got molded with regional and traditional motifs and assumed a new form. It soon become the most favorable art in the world of entertainment. But the Moslem religion forbade half-naked women to dance before men unknown to them. We must indicate, that only gypsies and non-Moslem women could break the rules only partly and in village weddings and holy days when entertainment was customary.

Dancer in the harem.

Even non-Moslem women were not allowed to dance everywhere before men. But people are intrinsically inclined to enjoy themselves and they soon found ways out of this situation. *chengis* who were women dancers began to entertain womenfolk and *köcheks* who were male dancers did the same for a male audience. *chengis* and *köcheks* conquered many hearts with their passionate dances 'cause oriental dance rests on the show of passion and fiery longing.

Let us give some short information on the different groups of dance to make the topic more tangible.

İt is possible to categorize Turkish dances into four main groups which are:

1. Religious Dances
2. Turkish Folk Dances
3. Modern Dances
4. Classical Dances

RELIGIOUS DANCES

This type of dance which was a part of religious rituals still exists in the modern Turkish society. 99% of the Turkish population is Moslem and there are many sects with different rituals. Some of these sects have adopted dance as a main characteristic of their ceremonies.

Mevlâna whirls in dance at the marketplace in Konya. Miniature from the 16th century.

The most renowned of the religious dances in Turkey is the "sema prayers" of the Mevlevid sect which was founded by Mevlâna Celaleddin Rumi (1207-1275) in Konya (antique *Iconium*).

A legend tells us, that Mevlana Celaleddin heard the hammer clang of a blacksmith as he was walking in the market place in Konya and began to whirl. It gives us the clue to the harmony of rhythm and dance. Mevlâna's whirl which was perfected after his death and adopted by the Mevlevi sect as the primary form of the unison with God is called *sema* (the sky).

The characteristic instrument of the Mevlevi worship rituals is called *ney*, a pipe made of reeds. The other known instruments are the *kuddüm* and *tambur* as percussion instruments and the *ud* and *kemenche* which are string instruments.

The *sema* dance takes place in a large hall of the dervish lodge (*tekke*), called the "semahane" (house of sema). *Sema* rituals are held especially on the holy nights of Islam *(kandil)*, on Friday and on December 17, which is the anniversary of Mevlâna's death. Many prayers are spoken and rituals are fulfilled in such nights and then the dancers, called "*semazen*," take their places in the hall and begin to whirl upon the permission of the sheikh.

There is always a chief who leads the dance of the *semazens*. They begin to dance to the specific music which the chief signals to start.

The *semazens* who wear white have always been men. However, recently women have also started to perform this dance in their colorful dresses. The dancers start to whirl on the spot where they stand. Their heads are always tilted a little to the right shoulder. The right hand is lifted towards the sky with the palm looking upwards. The left hand is directed down with the palm facing the earth. The *semazens* whirl to a mystical music which is intensified with the specific instruments we have

Whirling dervishes.

cited above. This dancing position is the symbol of the Mevlevis' interpretation of life and death: The position of the hands means, that we come from God and go to the earth, as well as, we take from God and give to man or we are a bridge between God and man. The sheikh who dances at the center symbolizes the sun which illuminates the universe, the *semazens* who whirl around him stand for the planets revolving around the sun, and their white vestures symbolize the godly universe and the world of spirits. The Anatolian peninsula is home to quite a number of beliefs two of which are the Alevi and Bektashi sects of Islam. The Bektashi sect was founded by Haci Bektaş Veli (1210-1271) who had immigrated to Anatolia from Harezm in the 13th century. It is a humanitarian sect which places man in the center of things and attributes all the good qualities to him. It is possible to summarize this sect's basic point-of-view as, "Be the master of your hand, your tongue and your belly," and "My Kaaba is man himself." The Bektashi sect, which adopted a much more human outlook compared to the rigid principles of Islam, is perceived to be a heretical one by the other sects of Islam. The Bektashi sect values poetry and music above all, reciting poetry accompanied by music and praising the humanistic attitude with their poetry. They have practiced their religious dance, called *sema* secretively for a long time in the past. The *sema* is a religious dance which either only men or men and women together practice. It is a part of the musical ceremony which they held in the Bektashi lodges and regarded to be the accompaniment of friendly talks.

The dancers form a circle and turn constantly with rhythmic foot movements; they move their hands and arms but never break the circle. They utter wise sentences which are more important than music at that instant. It has been discovered, that this dance also existed in Central Asia and was brought to Anatolia. The words *sema* and sema (sky) are so akin, that the common origin of these two dances is clear[2].

28

Turkish Folk Dances

The regional folk dances in Turkey are traditional dances which are natural to rural areas as they are everywhere else in the world. There are almost 2,000 regional folk dances in Turkey which extends over the Anatolian peninsula that has housed many cultures and still nourishes their residue.

The folk dances practiced in the east, west, north and south of the country vary a lot in clothing, melody, rhythm and choreography. One of the reasons for such a wide variety is the cultural heritage of the religious practices of the ancient peoples who have lived here. The dances which the Turks brought with them got intertwined with regional colors and Central Asian

Turkish folk dance from Giresun at the Black Sea coast.

Turkish folk dance from Giresun.

culture is reflected in them. Anatolian folk dances are dances which the locals perform on their joyful days and after the harvest. And some war dances have turned into folk dances in time.

Folk dances have different types which are either performed by men or a group of women or are danced together. Although Islam forbids men and women to dance together in public, many of the Turkish folk dances are performed together due to ancient Turkish traditions in Islamic Turkey.

Folk dances are danced to regional folk music. The big drum is a traditional instrument and accompanies almost all dances. Instruments like a single-reed wind instrument (*zurna*), the Turkish lute (*saz*), a small violin-like instrument (*kemenche*), the violin, tambourine (*tef*), the clarinet, the Turkish bagpipe (*tulum*) and the accordion are also common.

People who get together for engagement and circumcision ceremonies, weddings and other celebrations express their happiness through dance. Geographical remoteness is the main reason for the dance rhythms to differ so much. The people of the Black Sea coast dance their lively *horon*; whereas, the locals of Erzurum on the high plateaus dance their rather slow *bar*. The Aegean coast has its "*zeybek*" with costumes which reach as far back as Bacchus[3].

The variety of folk dances which can be grouped as *Halay* (Chain dance), *Karshilama* (Greetings), *Zeybek* and *Ağirlama* (Accommodating) are danced with a different choreography and music in different regions. The Turks generally prefer to dance their traditional folk dances. Even the people who immigrate to the large cities continue to perform their regional dances. A dance called *Chiftetelli* (with double strings) which has its roots in the classical *chengi* dances of old is the most widely practiced one. Turks call it belly dancing which derives from *Chiftetelli* and never conclude a celebration without it.

31

Sibel Gökçe dances " chiftetelli" (note the Turkish castanets in her hands).

MODERN DANCES

All the modern international dances are practiced in Turkey today. Advanced communication technology enables all age groups to keep in pace with the world, and especially the youngsters do not fall behind the global scene. This makes the discos the most "in" places which they prefer.

The Ottoman Empire began establishing closer relationships with the western countries since the end of the 18th century and gradually adopted the modern way of living. The westernization process lead to transformations in the lifestyle and traditions of the people but also in the economic downfall of the empire. Almost every sultan tried hard to save the empire by introducing decress which were thought to modernize the existing system. Western dances also appeared at the Ottoman palace during the same years. Historians teach us, that Selim III had watched the daughters of the French ambassador dance in the harem secretively and ordered his concubines to learn that kind of dance immediately. The first advertisements placed by dance teachers appeared in a daily paper in Istanbul in 1898. Levantines and Christian minorities became their students.

Revue stars began to dance at the night clubs in Beyoğlu (Pera) at the beginning of the 20th century and became an example for dance enthusiasts. The rich Moslem population soon developed an interest in the western style of dancing. Dances like the waltz, polka and quadrille became the *de rigour* of balls in 1905-1923.

The first tango orchestra was established in 1925. The foundation of the Turkish Republic in 1923 and further westernization led to the adoption of a western lifestyle as well as better relationships with the European countries. The interest in modern dance increased steadily and the ballet and modern ballet developed after 1935.

CLASSICAL DANCES

Turkish classical dances are oriental dances which the *chengis* and *köcheks* performed. Those are also the dances which gave rise to the belly dance which we know today.

Let us now indulge in the colorful world of the *chengis* and *köcheks*, and take a look at the glorious past of a dream world.

THE CHENGIS

The unforgettable female dancers of the east were called *chengis* and they were the stars of the Ottoman world of entertainment. There are two hypotheses which try to clarify the root of the word *chengi*: One of them says, that the word derives from "chang" which was a harp-like instrument, and the other one takes the word back to "chingene," meaning gypsy in Turkish, since the *chengis* were mostly gypsies.

Both hypotheses may hold true: The instrument and the dancer belong to each other indeed. The gypsies settled in Istanbul after Sultan Mehmet II conquered the city in 1453. Since the majority of these dancers were gypsies, the name *chengi* may have derived from them. The gypsies had adopted the Islamic belief but were rather reluctant to obey its rules. They preserved their own traditions instead. The *chengis* worked as organized groups and were the pillars of the entertainment world. A *chengi* group was called *kol* (troupe). Each *chengi* troupe comprised of a chief, her aide and 12 dancers. A group of musicians, called *siraci* (person in the row) accompanied the dancers. The four musicians who played two tambourines, a violin and a small double drum with sticks were also women.

The chief of the group was a *chengi* herself and was generally

Chengi. Levni's miniature from the 17th century.

Chengi in the harem.

a woman who knew the ways of the world. The chief was generally a lesbian who delighted in her group. Young and pretty girls, who wanted to become *chengis* and those who wanted to be perfect in their profession were tutored by the lesbian chief. The aide of the chief was most likely a middle-aged woman. It was customary for the aide to do the first dance called "the slow dance."

The chief's house was a rather enjoyable place full of young,

Chengi dancing in the harem.

beautiful and light girls where joyous music poured out of the
windows. It was a place which attracted the neighbors' attention.
Young men looking for enjoyment and well-to-do womanizers
clustered around such houses but it was only very seldom, that
*chengi*s had a good time with men. *Chengi* girls had love affairs
with their own sex and only some of them delighted in both
sexes. They generally preferred the members of their own sex
who had peaches-and-cream complexions and rosy lips. In

37

A chengi troupe performing at a wedding.

short, Ottoman *chengis* were renowned for their unabashed lesbianism.

The most famous *chengis* of Istanbul waited for invitations in Tahtakale (a district to the south of the Covered Bazaar) and in the gypsy quarter on the shores of the Golden Horn.

Women who organized a party at the public bath and those who held a ceremony of some sort bargained with the chief *chengi* and hired the group for the affair. As they bargained, they also decided whether the *chengis* would be free to collect tips after the entertainment was over. Some old and rich hostesses did not allow them to collect tips because they believed that it would disturb their guests. But women who liked the girls and their performance and danced along with them did give them tips or stuck gold coins on their foreheads. This tradition is still alive and belly dancers flow among the tables to collect tips. In the old days, the hostess of the ceremony had to tip them.

The scene of *chengis* walking in the street was an affair everyone wanted to see. The *chengi* group walked with their chief in the front who led the procession. The chief was veiled, wore yellow boots and held a fan in her hand. She walked with her aide beside her. The dainty and beautiful girls wrapped up in colorful street cloths (charshaf) and wearing thin veils followed them. They were followed by the musicians who carried their instruments in their cases, the maids and female porters who toted the costumes. In short, a queue of beauties made its appearance on the street.

As the coquettish beauties walked, they threw inviting glances at the men who followed them, winked at their admirers and petals of shrill laughter filled the skies. The *chengis* and a line of people after them signalled at each other, exchanged remarks secretively and arrived at the house where they were to show their talents. The hostess of the house always had a room at the first floor put at their disposal. The dancers retreated there to change their outfits.

It was absolutely forbidden to enter the dancers' room but a few and curious women did not refrain from using the keyhole to peep in.

People gossiped a lot about the dancers and said that they drank alcohol before the performance. They said locking up the door served this secret purpose. The dancers changed their outfits, put on their dancing costumes, powdered their faces, put on coal eye-liners and fake moles on their faces.

After they were finished with their make-up, their maid in charge of dresses helped them comb their hair, wear tulle shirts and sleeveless velvet jackets over them and wide skirts made of fine taffeta. Their skirts were decorated with gold fringes and a gilded belt completed the outfit. They wore special slippers for

Chengi dancing in the harem.

dancing, called *filer* and tied them over their white socks.

The chief of the group wore a more ladylike outfit. She took part in the dance only if she wore her dancing dress. After the *chengis* got dressed and ready, the musicians entered the room and took their place. The guests seated themselves on the chairs and some of them leaned on the big cushions on the floor, waiting eagerly for the show to begin. The musicians usually sang opening songs to warm up the audience waiting in anticipation for the dance to follow. The chief of the troupe and her aide saluted the guests in the room and walked around in the hall to greet them. This going around was called "slow tempo." The women who did the slow tempo did it rather slowly with their bodies naturally erect, arms held up and with cymballed tambourines in their hands. They walked around the room four times, meaning "we take so much zest out of it" (Turkish idiom: we have become four-cornered out of pleasure). This whole ceremony was the initial part of the session.

When the second part began, the dancers took to dancing with cymbals attached to their fingertips. It was done under the supervision of the chief, but the chief and her aide did not dance themselves. This was the most eloquent part of the oriental dance. The *chengis* swiveled their bellies, shook their hips and shoulders, jumped, galloped, beat the floor with their heels, swayed their necks either alone or in groups and caused many guests sigh with delight.

The third part was called "rabbit dance" and the *chengis* changed their dresses for it. They still had cymbals in their hands but changed to masculine baggy pants with matching sleeveless jackets, wrapped a shawl around their waists and wore a fez on the head without a turban. This part had a lot of hopping figures which reminded of a rabbit's walk and this choreographic detail rendered it its name.

Some rich ladies had an apple of the eye among the "*chengis.*" During the dance, those ladies and the dancers exchanged secret glances, signs and sighs and told each other secrets as the ladies granted gold coins to their paramours. The people sitting around perceived this closeness and many a relationship was clouded by jealous looks. The rivalry among women increased as more and more gold coins got stuck on the *chengi*'s forehead. They displayed their jealousy with deep sighs and dainty little remarks. The dancers and musicians exchanged improvised poems and songs, and the girls danced to their music like birds. They moved their feet so swiftly, that it became impossible to follow them. As the musicians exclaimed, "Oh, c'mon!," "Do it well!" and the like, both the dancers and the spectators flushed with merriment.

Sébah & Joa

The tempo of the dance increased with the applause. The *chengis* ended the third part by dancing in pairs. The fourth part was without dancing; *chengis* with a pleasant voice sang tunes to the music of the troupe. They sang in a shrill note and chose seductive songs. The spectators in the room lost their heads over the *chengis'* erotic voices and equally erotic words. They finished the fourth part with little dramatized games, for example, they imitated sailors in men's clothes. The imitation of men excited and charmed their audience. The program ended with the public bath game: The *chengi* dressed as a male merchant made as if she passed by a bath and called out to his lover inside, singing doleful love songs. And this scene fascinated the ladies. *Chengi* performances usually started in the early evening and lasted till daybreak[(4)].

Chengis also performed in the public baths for women when the latter organized a "women's day." Their job would be to guarantee the ladies a jolly time in the bath. This time, the erotic dances of the half-naked *chengis* made them dizzy with fever.

Lots of poems and stories have been written on the *chengis* who were the stars of the Ottoman world of entertainment. Renowned *chengis* became the theme of many a song and thus conquered the hearts.

Chengis were identified with entertainment in the Ottoman palaces too. In the Ottoman Empire, which used to be one of the mightiest empires in history, some of the concubines bought for the harem of the sultan's palace were trained in music and singing. Those who were talented were trained in dancing. Tutors who came from abroad taught these young girls not only *chengi* dances but also Andalusian ones. In the end, some of the concubines were kept only for such talents. They were the stars in the sultan's *halvet* (privacy) nights and tried to win his heart with their most sensuous dances. Some of those dancers even managed to become sultans' wives. And still some sultans had

Chengis.

the renowned *chengi*s of the city invited to the palace for special nights and granted them handfuls of gold after the performance.

There were also *chengi*s or dancers who were sent to the capital from such imperial lands as Egypt, Palestine and North Africa. Those girls did not only become dancers in the palace but also concubines in the mansions of the rich. Such concubines became chiefs of *chengi* troupes in their old age. Women of the harem also invited *chengi*s for entertainment and it was a pleasure for them to sway their bodies before the privileged harem population. Historians tell us, that *chengi* troupes made colorful performances at the famous Ottoman festivities which were held to celebrate lady sultans' weddings or the heirs' circumcision ceremonies. Turkish *chengi*s danced even at a festival that the Italians organized in 1524. *Chengi*s

45

Musicians in the harem.
Levni's miniature from the 17th century.

were also present at the festivities in 1530 and 1539. But since all the dancers were called *chengi* in those years, the dancers who danced in public at the festivities must have been men and not women. In short, we can assume, that all social classes liked and enjoyed the magic of oriental dancing.

The *chengi*s began to light up men's special nights of entertainment towards the end of the 19th century.

Ahmet Mithat Efendi narrated the performance of a group of three *chengi*s at a private night in his book, *chengi* in the following realistic tone:

"One of the *chengi*s whose name was Sümbül wore a *chengi* costume made of pink satin. Arife's dress was of blue satin and Nazli wore one of black satin which she also knew how much it suited her. Sümbül and Arife had small, shiny discs sewn on their costumes symmetrically; whereas, the ones on Nazli's dress were thrown on it at random and that style looked very pretty indeed.

When they began to dance with moderate movements totally

46

in accord with the music, being neither fast and shrill nor devoid of a soft harmony, all the spectators really paid deep attention to the artistic movements of these three women. When they approached the men for whom they wished to make themselves desirable, the shoulders, arms, wrists and tits began to tremble like the other parts of their bodies as if they were tied to their places with springs; and they practiced their profession with all their courage as if they needed strong feet in order to control their beautifully twitching bodies. In the meantime, armfuls of hair which extended below the waists could not be tamed because of those vibrating bodies either. As they covered their faces to avoid the lovers who yearned for them, they held those clusters of hair with tiny delicate fingers which could hardly grasp the cymbals, and threw them over their shoulders with such a beautiful and pretended anger, that the hearts of eager lovers were more triggered by this action than by the rest.

The *chengis* did this special movement in front of their admirers for only a couple of moments and never longer. The second they realized that the craving lover was about to embrace them with valor, those coquettes in shimmering dresses turned around their own axis just like revolving spheres and disappeared immediately. Having retreated enough, they put on a very delicate and a little obscene smile and applauded the poor lovers' craving.

But some other crafts are needed if the poor lover is to be kept on the taught string between sadness and expectation, and those flirtatious restrictions were the *chengis'* mastership. Those three women were undoubtedly unsurpassed in this exercise. After she fulfilled all the minute

delicacies of this art, she almost covered her face with the back of her right hand as if she were ashamed of her previous heartlessness, kept the cymbals still and looked at her lover with languid eyes as she then uncovered her face. Bringing that right

Chengis. End of the 19th century.

hand backwards towards her belly and balancing her own body
on it revealed her naked neck which shone like a silver sea, and
when she pulled kisses from her own cherry lips to throw at her
admirer, the poor lover forgave all the feigned reluctance and
whims, and would do the same even if they were not pretended.

Then, the guests begged Sümbül to dance alone.

Her specific tune began to pour out of the instruments and
she took off the old cymbals on her fingers and put on her

A chengi troupe. End of the 19th century.

special ones. Sümbül began to dance to a fast melody. She started to turn around in a fashion which made it necessary to say, "those who want to see a person fly, should see Sümbül" because saying, "this is what is called dancing" would not suffice.

Trembling and shaking the belly would have looked absolutely cheap and ugly in her dance, and had she condescended to exercise that vulgar side of her profession, there would have been no one to praise her. Her tiny feet which the white, only knee-long dress could not conceal touched the floor solely at the toe tips. But since she changed her position very briskly, the tips of her toes could not be seen touching the ground and the woman looked as if she danced in the air. You should not assume after our description of her very fast movements, that an excited flutter had taken hold of her body above the waist, and that it was not a very nice sight to look at. Sümbül's body is composed of an upper part and a separate lower one which are maybe tied to each other by the belly. Can this be possible? Though she touched the ground with a point at her foot at a speed of one thousand times per second but still looked as if she didn't, her torso above the waist swayed like that of a tall youngster whose beautiful sweep made the eyes gleam, and every part of her upper body drove everyone crazy with beautiful movements in a minute. One of her feet became the center of a circle and the other one drew its circumference by a slow turn...This artistic show, which couldn't even be rightfully described by the most talented pen, stupefied everyone present in the room."[5]

The *chengi* profession lost its former glory at the beginning of the 20th century. The turn of the century marked the period of decline of the Ottoman Empire. Wars, defeats, economic problems and a general pessimism disabled the society and therefore their previous ways of amusement.

Economic decline became an obstacle for the *chengi* troupes who worked with a lot of dancers. Such groups diminished to only three or four dancers and a few musicians under the supervision of a chief. The downfall of the economy in general also led to the economic upsurge of the Levantines and Christian minorities who demanded not the traditional but the western ways of amusement. Consequently, European show stars began to replace the traditional dancers.

The "kanto" singers and revue stars became public darlings in Pera which was the throbbing heart of the entertainment world at the turn of the century. Even the Palace paid great attention to them and it did not take long for those stars to become the heroines of many love affairs.

Chengi.

A chengi troupe. End of the 19th century.

ORGIES WITH DRINK AND WOMEN DANCERS & MERRYMAKING

Another type of dance similar to the classical *chengi* and *köchek* dances still exists in some parts of Anatolia today. This type of gathering was called *oturak* (orgy with drink and women dancers) in the Konya region, and bore the name *cümbüsh* (merrymaking) in Ankara and its surroundings. This performance was like the kind of modern belly dancing we know today and was organized by men in secret at night. Generally, the merchants and higher officials in towns got together for entertainment in a house which was located away from downtown.

They usually called a single woman dancer to the gathering. She offered drinks to the spectators, sang songs and then belly danced with cymbals on her fingertips. The dancer always had a protector called "Efe" and he also joined in if the hosts invited him.

Oturak or *cümbüsh* nights had strict rules, the most important of which was "No molesting the dancer." It was even forbidden to look above the waistline of the dancers during *cümbüsh* nights. Some of the spectators made music at such gatherings.

Hosts preferred dancers who were good at chiming the cymbals and playing an instrument called the *cümbüsh*, which resembles a banjo. The dancer performing at an orgy began her dance in a rather covering outfit but then stripped slowly as the fun increased, so that she looked scantily dressed in the end[6].

Such nights of merriment were held in secret because of public dislike. This performance, which actually derived from the Bacchanalian feasts of Anatolian antiquity, came to be practiced in secret because of a Moslem society's moralistic control and its sensuous taste was not emphasized. But allowing men to watch the dancer only up until the waistline during *cümbüsh* nights is adequate evidence for regarding her to be just a sex object.

THE KÖCHEKS

Islam forbids women to dance in front of men openly because such an act is thought to be immoral, but of course there are no restrictions if it is done behind closed doors and in private property. Inspite of religious pressures, Ottomans have always wanted to share the jollity of feasts and the zest of dancing together with women. They tackled this problem with the emergence of male dancers called *köcheks*. We come across them in the chronicles starting with the 15th century. Foreign travellers have written over them and introduced them to us as seductive dancers who triggered the spectator's lust, and who were favored very much by the public.

In his "Book of Travels," Evliya Çelebi wrote the following on the *köchek* groups in Istanbul: "Whenever there is a sultan's wedding or a celebration following a conquest, or a nobility wedding or circumcision ceremony in Istanbul; singers, dancers, drum players, clowns, imitators and experienced city boys get together and dance a day and night long, or for two days or five, and get a pouchful of Kurush from the host as tip every night. There are masters who go around eager and enjoyment-seeking participants with a tambourine in their hands and pocket as much as one thousand Kurush at a wedding in a single night. They number almost three hundred and their classes are called 'branch.' They are a class worthy of watching. This group of professionals has 12 branches."

Evliya Çelebi wrote about each of these branches and we will give two of them below:

"The 'Zümrüt Branch' (emerald): It has 300 men. The Greeks, Armenians and city boys of Yedikule, Narlikapi and Sulumanastir have come together to form a branch. But of the dancers; curly-haired, doe-eyed and long-lashed Dimitraki, Neferaki and Yanaki of Chios are the best *köcheks* who have set

Köchek dancing in an inn.

Istanbul on fire and spent the treasures of many an admirer, causing them to fall prey to deep poverty.

The 'Çelebi Branch' (refined): It has 200 men. The most beautiful of the dancers are: Can Memi, Zalim Shah, Hürrem Shah, Fitne Shah and Yusuf Shah. And Circassian Mirza Shah surpasses the angels in beauty. These boys became famous in Istanbul, and have even danced before Sultan Murat IV who granted them a lot of money.

The *köchek*s did belly dancing in women's clothes.

*Köchek*s were always sensuous, attractive and effeminate youngsters who were carefully selected and trained. They started

A köchek troupe performing at an Ottoman festivity.

schooling at a very young age, got trained in music and dance, and learned the secrets of the profession from older and experienced mentors. They were the apples of the eye in the Ottoman world of entertainment. They danced in public gardens, weddings, feasts, festivals, and in the presence of sultans.

Besides those who danced in women's clothes, there were also some *köchek*s who wore baggy pants when they danced. They were called Rabbit Boys who wore black pants made of broadcloth and silk shirts and tied a sash around the waist. Their outfit always revealed the figure in it. Even the concubines

A köchek troupe performing at an Ottoman festivity.

Köcheks.

in the harem wore such pants and imitated the dance of the Rabbit Boys when they wanted to entertain themselves.

The *köchek*s wore gold-embroidered velvet shirts generally, and their silk skirts had fringes that matched with the belt. They had curly long hair, wore exotic perfumes and were made up like women.

They danced with castanets (çalpara) in their hands and clapped them to the tempo of the melody. They began to use cymbals later on. The *köchek*s danced a sexually provocative oriental dance to oriental music and to a fast and agile type of composition called "*köchekche*."

The way they shook their belly, threw their hair back, jumped on their toetips, quivered their shoulders, and even imitated sexual intercourse with their movements aroused the sensual feelings of their spectators.

The *köchek*s walked around the dancing spot before the music began and threw inviting glances and bashful smiles at their admirers. The ladylike way they walked and their whimsical expressions incited their guests' hearts. They sometimes danced fully dressed like women whereby no one could tell the difference between the sexes, and in such cases, the air would overflow with "oh"s and "ah"s and the wind of lust would take hold of everyone. These beautiful male coquettes drove men crazy with their seductive sighs and oriental dance.

It was usual for the audience to shatter drinking glasses, to yell nasty words at each other and even to molest the dancers during that passionate dance. Those who were enchanted by oriental dancing could not free themselves from the *köchek*s' seductiveness. The boys' beauty would become the most important topic in town; people would gossip about their other talents(!), dedicate poems to them and compose yearning songs.

Some *köchek*s performed regularly in Istanbul's big coffee houses. Especially the drinking houses in Galata took care to keep *köchek*s at the disposal of their customers. The boys working there were clad as Rabbit Boys and also served drinks with coy mimics to make their customers blind drunk[8].

The *köchek*s were generally Gypsy, Jewish, Armenian, Greek or natives of the Isle of Chios. Most of them converted to Islam and took Turkish names, and almost all of them had nicknames which hinted at their special talents. The presence of the *köchek*s is a good example that shows how oriental dancing and sexuality overlap.

The *köchek* profession became out of date in the era of Sultan Mahmut II (1808-1839). It was banned by a firman which the sultan released upon Grand Vizier Reşit Pasha's insistence in 1856. Following this date, most of the *köchek*s emigrated to Egypt where Mehmet Ali Pasha ruled.

THE KÖCHEK TRADITION TODAY

Male dancers dressed as women still exist in places like Zonguldak, Bartin, Çankiri, Bolu and Safranbolu in northwest Anatolia. They perform only in weddings and on special celebration days. This profession is not organized in troupes like in the Ottoman times, has lost its sensual touch and acquired the characteristic of a popular game.

Boys of 12-13 get trained by an older *köchek*, learn how to dance and display their talents at some social gatherings. The trainers put the young boys in a basket which they hang down a ceiling and turn them around very fast, so that they get used to the most difficult figure. The drummers who accompany a *köchek*'s dance also make fast turns as they play and dance at the same time[9]. The oriental dance of young men who wear women's clothes is nothing but a folkloric show today.

Musicians and Dancer: Hittite relief 8th century B.C. (Ankara Museum of Anatolian Civilizations

THE ORIGINS OF THE ORIENTAL BELLY DANCE

Let us consider the origins of this type of dance before we take a glance at its characteristics. In all Middle Eastern countries including Turkey, gypsy dancers appear to be the axis in the history of belly dancing. Gypsies, who were an ancient people settled in India, left the Indian peninsula in the 5th century A.D and immigrated to the Middle East, the Mediterranean basin and Europe. They always lived in the suburbs of large cities and sustained themselves with simple jobs. They were always known for their talent and mastership in

Gypsy dancers in Sulukule/ İstanbul.

Mother Goddess statuettes. 6000 B.C. Museum of
Anatolian Civilizations in Ankara.

music and dance. This traditional inclination of the Gypsies
derived from their religious rituals back in India. Dancing and
sexuality are intrinsic to the Krishna and Tantra creeds. Gypsies
resisted discrimination in foreign lands with music, dance and
jollity. People who were dazzled by their talents and were
interested in watching their dances gradually wanted to do so by
paying a certain fee. This led to the emergence of professional
Gypsy dancers. But the Gypsy tradition alone falls short of
explicating the magic of oriental dance. It is impossible to
oversee its universal essence since it moves everybody from all
nations.

The first planned cities of mankind were established in the
Anatolian peninsula, Mesopotamia and the Middle East. Our
forefathers founded their cities mostly around temples which
they dedicated to their mother goddess who symbolized fertility,

abundance and in short, life.

Archaeological excavations made in late stone age cities like Çatalhöyük and Hacilar in Anatolia have revealed mother goddess statuettes with exaggerated breasts and hips and a pregnant look. The oldest mother goddess was called "Ma" in the ancient Anatolian languages. Man in the ancient times lived with the craving struggle for survival in an alien and unfriendly nature. And he lacked the knowledge and tools which would enable him to win the fight against nature. Thus, in an age when death was the main peril, it was only natural, that man would sanctify the female who gave birth and life to him.

Sexuality was the main theme and the ultimate aim in the religious feasts which were born from the mother goddess cult. Women served in the antique temples which had been erected to honor the mother goddess. They were the sacred priestesses (Anaitis) who united with the worshippers to be one with the mother goddess. The priestesses wore dresses fit for the religious ritual and danced in a way to arouse the worshippers with whom they had sexual intercourse afterwards. it would be realistic to say, that oriental dance has originated from the ancient priestesses' provocative dance for bodily unison.

Beliefs and traditions changed in the long course of human history. But in the Aegean and Mediterranean basins and in the Middle East where polytheist beliefs had followed the cult of the mother goddess, dance continued to be a part of the religious rituals.

Sacred intercourse conducted on behalf of the mother goddess reappears a lot later in the Bacchanalian feasts held in Anatolia. In the feasts held in honor of the wine god Bacchus, men and women danced ritual dances and had sexual intercourse with each other in a state of ecstacy.

There used to be a similar belief among the people of Canaan in Israel who held "Tebernace" feasts. They, too, danced till daybreak and engaged in random sexual intercourse.

The priestesses in the temples of Aphrodite in ancient Greece indulged in a kind of sacred prostitution. Young slave girls who were bought for the temple slept with worshippers and were thought to be liaisions between the mortals and the goddess.

Monotheist religions banned dancing because they evaluated it as a form of polytheist worship. But the nature of man, that is, his sexuality cannot be suppressed for long although civilian and canonic rules served to conceal the sensuous dimension of any dance. In the end, dance as a way of sexual invitation continued to live in spite of modifications that harmonized with socially acceptable behaviour.

The sexually provocative dance got modified according to traditions, religious rules and regional music and dances; in other words, it got tamed and became the oriental belly dance. This new form was socially agreeable but it was not possible to cover up its sexual implications. Behavioral similarities in geographical regions hint at common cultural histories as well as multilateral influences. Although oriental belly dance is practiced in a wide area, we can say that the stylistic differences we see in the Middle East and North Africa are the results of regional folkloric elements. Oriental belly dance is the artistic expression of man's innate instinct to reproduce reflected in the female's rhythmic movements.

Even the name of the dance insinuates at the sensuality which is always hidden in it. In ancient times, dancing priestesses also displayed man's natural history; they mimicked sexual intercourse, pregnancy, birth, the joy of birth, breastfeeding and protection with their dancing limbs. Oriental belly dance also has traces of those ancient movements which told man's story. When the dancer turns her back to the onlooker and swings her hips, she sends a message which can be interpreted as the call for copulation.

Rezzan, an oriental dancer
famous in the 70's.

In prehistoric times, human beings imitated the animals when they engaged in sexual intercourse, and the male positioned himself behind the female during the sexual act. There is a witness for this ancient method; it is the "Bitik Vase" which dates back to the Early Hittite Age and is now in the Museum of Anatolian Civilizations in Ankara. The Hittites have pictured all the scenes of a wedding ceremony as frescoes on the surface of a relatively big vase. The scene of the nuptial night shows the bride bending and the groom approaching her from behind. The swinging hips and the quivers seen in oriental belly dance are nothing but the imitation of intercourse and orgasm.

Jerking the belly, which is the most important figure, is the imitation of the fetal kicks, and symbolizes pregnancy. The figure where the dancer kneels on the floor with her knees touching it, spreads her legs and moves her hips up and down gives enough clues for a mimicked delivery. Thrusting the breasts forwards and shaking them hints at the milk and child feeding. And finally, when the dancer embraces her own body with her arms, the act symbolizes motherly protection for the infant.

Many movements of the dancer reflect the respect which was once shown to the mother goddess. The way the dancer stands between positions, some bends of the body, and especially the hand movements derive from the worshipping ritual. But the spectator registers all of these as figures which increase his lust. Spiritual changes like the birth of monotheist religions and social ones like masculine hegemony have influenced and changed the role and position of women in society. Such transformations led to the disappearance of mother goddesses and women lost their sacred position in society, becoming sexual objects of men under their overpowering role. They lost the respect which had taken its roots from the female's ability to create. Oriental dance became a tool for women's personal

Actress Fatma Girik as an oriental dancer.

rehabilitation in the Middle Ages when women suffered most from social limitations. Thus, the oriental dancer supported herself financially, became the center of attraction, and had relatively more personal freedom than the other members of her sex. The dancer preserved this status from the Middle Ages until the beginning of the 20th century. Today, oriental dance stands wide apart from its original meaning but preserves the sexual message as its core.

Although Oriental Belly Dance denotes a regional description, it attracts and appeals to people both in the east and in the west and mystifies them equally. The real reason for this appeal is nothing less than man's innate tendency for reproduction.

Another reason for the spectators to watch this dance almost in a trance is maybe that ancient inclination to dance as a part of religious rituals. It is as if the admirers of oriental belly dance set out on a long journey in time. The call to sexual intercourse which was done in the name of mother goddesses 8,000 years ago still gets hold of men and women alike.

Oriental dance enables flashbacks of some eastern women like Cleopatra, Semiramis, the Queen of Sheba, Salome, Empress Theodora, the concubines in sultans' harems and the voluptuous females of the tales in "1001 Nights," whose sensuality and sex appeal have always been exaggerated, and such characters suddenly "appear" on the dancing floor as the modern dancer begins to swivel her hips. This magnificent jump in time intensifies the dancer's magic which hangs in the air. This illusion is another reason for the general appreciation of the oriental belly dance.

Princess Banu, beautiful anf famous dancer loved by the public.

CHARACTERISTICS OF TURKISH BELLY DANCING

Belly Dancing, which is a professional show branch, which has continued for many years in Turkey, carries forth the existence of the Turkish society with all its exuberance.

The proclamation of the Turkish Republic in 1923 and the establishment of the secular state granted great freedom to belly dancers just as it has liberated all women in many aspects of communal life. Turkish belly dancers began to enjoy a kind of freedom they could never have dreamt of having in the Ottoman Period. They stopped being members in *chengi* troupes and picked up belly dancing to go on and become show stars. The first Turkish woman dancer performed on stage in 1919 and was the cause celebré for major reactions.

Dancers, who were able to perform on stage quite easily during the Republican Era, found opportunities for themselves to dance as they wished and select their outfits freely. As a consequence of this development, Turkish belly dancing flourished in a way to display nude feminine beauty and underline sexual appeal in a covert manner. Turkish dancers perform a style of Oriental Belly Dancing that appeals to the eyes and soul much more than the dancers in Moslem countries of the Middle East and North Africa. This is one of the reasons why Turkish dancers are invited to perform so often to these countries.

The Turkish people are smitten with beauty and take young belly dancers who are brunettes, brown-haired, blondes, nice-faced, plumpish figured and frisky into their hearts. Turkish belly dancers have acquired the name "Turkish delight" all around the world, referring to the famous Turkish sweet which is just as delicious. They have been accepted by the Turkish

Inci Birol.

Mehtap Deniz.

society as sexual idols because they put their sexuality in the foregound. furthermore, see in them the infamous "femme fatale" or the "fickle female" who has had a checkered history as the anti-heroine character in Turkish film.

The biggest danger facing Turkish Oriental dancers today is the fact that they are involved in a struggle against the morals of a Moslem country as well as being under the pressure which arises from being sex symbols.

Though the secular Turkish Republic has eased women's lives

Turkish belly dancer.

extremely, granting them civil liberties that only men had enjoyed before, it can only lighten the social pressures to a certain extent. The conflict which continues between sexuality and social moral values gives shape to the appearance and content of Oriental Dance in several countries.

As long as Turkish dancers continue to stake a claim to their liberties, they will always find the power in themselves to emphasize the sexual dimension in Oriental Dancing.

Turkish dancers insist that their profession falls within the framework of the performance arts. Yes, belly dancing is an art indeed. There are hundreds of Turkish musical masterpieces that were composed especially for this art. It requires lots of creativity to design costumes for belly dancers who are not only experienced practitioners but also imaginative creators.

The Oriental Belly Dance is a lyrical performance which reveals the feminine beauty and feelings through body language expressed in a choreographic order. It is a way for a woman to express herself; it is indeed the female herself as much as it is tangible love itself. The belly dance is nourished by that ancient instinct of man, that is, sexuality per se.

Sexuality is overtly offered in Turkish belly dancing and the dancer cannot help being regarded as a sexual object.

There are some critics who evaluate the oriental belly dance as an imported art and not as a genuinely Turkish one. But it exists in this country since at least 500 years. Turkey is a country which also comprises oriental motifs and it must not be disregarded, that oriental belly dancing has formed on this sunny soil.

It is performed in all eastern countries since hundreds of years too, but the Turkish belly dance is a genuine composition which has acquired its latest form after many modifications due to the Turks' traditions and taste. Just as we refer to the Turkish Football, Turkish Television, Turkish cars, Turkish architecture and the Turkish theater, it is only natural to talk about a Turkish belly dance which has a specific form in this country. Moreover, its history is much older than the other entities we have cited above.

The Turkish belly dance is an original Turkish dance. It is also a classical Turkish dance. Turkish belly dancers are favored not only in the world in general, but also in the Arab countries because theirs is a specially Turkish composition underlining sexuality and local motifs.

URKISH DELIGHT   SEMIRE SEMIR

Nilüfer Aydan.

An alternative to the Turkish belly dancer is the Egyptian one who has to suppress the sexual content of the dance to the utmost because of social ethics. The sexual appeal of belly dancing has been replaced by a tamed theatrical performance in Islamic countries such as Egypt, Kuwait, Morocco, Tunisia and Algeria. In these countries, it is performed at a further distance away from the spectator and keeps him away. It looks like the gymnastics of the limbs accompanied by hip movements done to

Aysel Tanju, the symbol of voluptousness.

an oriental rhythm. An Egyptian belly dancer can stay on the platform for 2-2,5 hours which is a long span of time enabled by her slowness and relative inactivity. For this reason, as far as the occupation is concerned, by the time they reach their sixties, they are considered to have finally hit the age of maturity On

Harry Belafonte admiring   79
Saliha Tekneci.

the contrary, the Turkish belly dancer dances in a sexually attractive, original style since the beginning. The Ottoman traditional dancing with its *chengi*s and *köchek*s has moulded her attitude of open sexual attractiveness. In other words, the past has determined the present also in Turkish belly dancing and has made the modern dancer the fulcrum of sexuality.

This is the most important characteristic of Turkish belly dancing. It is practiced in close proximity to the audience and draws the spectator into its sensual fire.

The Turkish belly dancer's program is composed of two parts. First, she dances and shows her talents, and then she comes closer to the audience and becomes a figure in the group, encouraging them to participate in her show. She makes her admirers meet with the magic of oriental dance. True to a tradition which extends back to the Ottoman times, she provokes the spectator for a tip, also giving him the chance to touch a goddess who has come from the depths of time.

The Turkish belly dancer invites some lucky spectators to dance with her, letting them become participants in that old sexual ritual. She turns the dance into an active show in which everybody rejoices.

Turkish belly dancing is loyal to the ancient sexual instinct and is replenished by classical Ottoman routines and local dances. Although it comprises some of the classical oriental routines practiced by dancers in Egypt, Arabia, North Africa, Andalusia and India, it has also moulded the routines of such classical dances as *Karshilama* (greeting), *Köchekche* (of the *köchek*s) and *Chiftetelli* (double-stringed). The music is uniquely Turkish. Dancers sometimes beat a tempo to a melody that is 150-200 years old with their cymbals, but they may also quiver their hips to a latest hit.

Turkish belly dancing, which rests on rich Anatolian dance motifs along with classical Indian and Arabian ones, is enriched

Famous belly dancer
Özel Türkbaş.

by an Ottoman past, and has reached a perfection in the freedom the secular Republic of Turkey has granted to it.

Turkish belly dancers dance faster and with more tempo than their colleagues in other countries and therefore, their programs are shorter. On the average, the Turkish belly dancer performs a routine that lasts 30-40 minutes, but some very experienced dancers extend their program and dance up to an hour.

Contrary to Egyptian Oriental Dance where the dancer stands in the spot, vibrating her hips, belly and shoulders like a snake, the Turkish dancer utilizes the whole place, spreading her movements into the whole room. She presents her program with special stances, hand and arm movements, the harmonious swaying of the body, belly shake, turning the neck, trembling the shoulders, kicking out the hips in tempo with the musical rhythm and the seductiveness of the eyes. It is only possible to see the flexibility and capacity of the female body by watching a Turkish belly dancer.

Mezdeke Belly Dance Group.
They never take off their veils.

ORIENTAL DANCERS

The majority of all belly dancers in all countries have been of Gypsy origin. We have already underlined the fact that the majority of all *chengi*s and *köchek*s were Gypsies in the Ottoman times as well. The ratio of Gypsy dancers has declined since the foundation of the Turkish Republic and many of the dancers are no longer of Gypsy origin.

Turkish belly dancers, white-skinned, a bit plump and of medium height, have been very successful on the stage since the 1930's.

An oriental dancer must be a bit on the plump side to be

Funda Yanar putting a spell on the crowd.

successful in trembling motions. Dancers are generally 1.65-1.75 m high. Their breasts measure 86-90 cm, their waist 58-64 cm and their hips 88-98 cm. These measurements are very close to those of the so-called ideal female measurements of 90-60-90 cm.

A skinny dancer does not have abundant chances to be successful and to be favored. The Turkish masculine taste favors well-shaped and plump dancers. Furthermore, a dancer's hair should hang down to her waist line, so that she can play with her hair as she dances.

Turks really believe in the proverb which says, "What makes a meal tasty is its sauce; for a woman it's her hair and her hips." And when Turkish belly dancers choose a top that's a little bit tight, so much the better for the spectator.

The majority of dancers performing in Turkey are dark-haired: Another Turkish proverb says, "The blonde has a name but the dark one has taste." Turkish dancers look very attractive and arousing with the contrast between their white skin and long dark hair. Shortly, the preferences of Turkish men have determined the physical looks of the dancers.

Young dancers who have chosen this profession are always tutored by older, experienced dancers or instructors. It is here that we should mention the male dancer, Kudret Şandra, who has tutored and prepared more than 500 belly dancers for the stage.

There are no institutions in Turkey where candidate dancers can receive training; therefore, it is becoming more difficult to preserve the features of Turkish Belly Dancing. There are only a few private courses where belly dancing is taught and their students mostly learn it for their own pleasure. Only a few of those students perform go on to dance professionally later. The real "school" of belly dancing are the Gypsies themselves who have performed this profession as *chengis* and *köcheks* since the

Dancer Ateş Yıldızı
(pseudonym meaning " fire star").

Princess Banu

15th century. The Gypsies, who live a secluded life in such places as Ayvansaray, Sulukuḷe and Selamsiz in Istanbul, have turned every home into a school and trained many renowned dancers, fulfilling their own tradition.

They still put on belly dancing exhibits in Sulukule today. They set up dinner tables for their guests at their homes and dance for cash. Those who wish to participate in such an entertainment should not forget to do so with the help of a guide and should be ready to tip the dancers abundantly. Otherwise, great disappointment in every sense of the word is almost sure to follow.

Gypsies have a special place in the Turkish world of entertainment either as dancers or as musicians. An old proverb introduces them as "people who have the capacity to dance even to the sound of a creaking door."

Kudret Şandra prepares Elife for the stage.

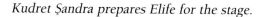

Sabine Sevan

Sedef Türkay (at the left) and Semra Nil (above).

Gypsy dancers before a Queen of Dancers contest.

Turkish belly dancers display their talents professionally at the "Queen of Belly Dancers" contest which is held annually. This contest has been held since the 1950's and has introduced many beloved dancers to the public. Not only does the contest give new dancers a chance to appear on stage, but it also encourages new routines to appear and enrich belly dancing in general.

Young dancers before a Queen of Dancers contest.

ORIENTAL DANCE MUSIC

Oriental belly dance is always accompanied by oriental music which is composed of tones that are very different from those of occidental music. Melodies called *köchekche*, "dance tune" and "broken tune" make up that Turkish belly dance music which is quite fast and vibrant. The oldest of these tunes are the *köchekches* which once used to accompany the dance of the *köchek*s.

A *köchekche* is composed of a number of phrases following each other with a binding movement in between. The *kemenche*, a string instrument resembling a smaller violin held upside down and the *lavta* which looked like a lute, were the two essential instruments to play *köchekches*.

The melody was a little bit brisk in the beginning and then the tempo became faster and the melody swifter. A binding tune

Oriental music troupe in Sulukule.

Semra Özge

Yüksel Şenkaya dancing under the " kanun" on her belly.

was played with the kemenche between the phrases. The
*köchek*che has become one of the tessituras of Turkish classical
music. Many renowned composers and even Sultan Selim III was
known to have composed fast *köchekches*.

Oriental belly dancers choose the melodies and make up their
own repertories according to their own taste and body
flexibility. However, there are professional music directors who
compose repertories too. Oriental dancers usually dance to
popular Turkish tunes especially composed for dancing because
the public is used to them and is moved by them. Some of these

Tülay Karaca with her musicians.

hits are *Bahriye Chiftetellisi*, *Ali Baba*, *Mevlâna* and *Chadirimin Üstüne*, tunes which every dancer has in her repertoire. Some dancers have also been dancing to *Arabesque* melodies recently.

Oriental dance music is the essential part of the dance which cannot be performed with occidental melodies.

Turkish music in general is so rich in rhythms, that it gives the dancer to exploit the full flexibility of her body, and to show all the intricate movements of her art. Oriental dance music is a kind of music which fills up and conquers the body, making it impatient with the longing to dance. It grows restless, begins to fidget and you start to twist and turn.

Turks take to dancing and showing their love of life almost immediately when they hear this type of music ooze from the instruments, and this holds true for both sexes. As soon as the music fills up their ears, the nerves of the body begin to twitch, kindling a revolt which bows to that brisk, colorful and swaying music.

Regardless of which eastern instruments are being played, the belly dancer always uses a small accessory for tempo which multiplies that sweet violence in the heart.

The *chengi*s and *köchek*s used a tempo instrument called *chalpara* as we have indicated before. *Chalparas* were made of two pairs of short wooden sticks and were extraordinarily good for the purpose. They can be clearly seen in the engravings and miniatures which are printed in this book. Some *köchek*s and *chengi*s were even famous with their ability to keep tempo with *chalparas* in their hands.

Modern Turkish belly dancers use small cymbals called *zil* which are two small brass discs with a radius of 6-7 cm. They are usually engraved on the outside and have loops made of short rubber bands. The dancer wears them on her fingers and clashes them to the beat of the music. Cymbals and dancers are life-long partners on the job. A dancer who dances without clinking the cymbals is considered to be either very inexperienced or else is no dancer at all.

The famous star, Princess Banu.

COSTUMES FOR ORIENTAL DANCING

Dancers look like they have stepped out of the Garden of Eden when they slide on the dancing floor wearing those colorful costumes. What makes a dancer so attractive is her costume on a beautifully chiselled body. Although dancing costumes are also sold off-the-rack, most dancers have their costumes designed and tailored for them.

The oriental dancer's costume always reveals something interesting, but it also has to conceal something vital. Exactly the right amount of covering up is necessary for the dancer to look familiar as well as like an outlaw who rises against all ethics. Their bras are traditionally very low-cut. A dancer's costume is mainly composed of a bra, underpants, tulle and fringes. Every dancer wears those costumes which she thinks are most suitable for her beauty, emphasizing the most attractive parts of her body. But all costumes have something in common: They tickle men's feelings...

Costumes for belly dancing are always lively with color; the most preferred ones being shades of red, light green, light blue, yellow and white, though white is used less often as it symbolizes purity. Bras and underpants are mostly embroidered with tiny beads and colorful metallic discs.

Dancers wear a kind of skirt made of tulle or fringes which they tie on the underpants with a belt. It depends solely on the dancer whether she will take off the belt or not. They usually appear on the stage with a wrap around the body and slowly take it out as they dance. Belly dancers also use veils or capes to hide away their bodies first and then to reveal their full beauty. Some dancers unite belly dancing with strip-tease and dress accordingly. They strip off the tulle pieces as they dance and

Beautiful Sibel Barış in a very attractive costume.

World famous Özel Türkbaş.

Mezdeke Belly Dance Group.

remain only with a bra and underpants.

There are more daring dancers too, who replace their bras with a handful of gold or silver powder stuck on their nipples. Or they replace the underpants with stockings and tie the belt on it. As the tulle or fringes sway to and fro, the hips and bowels become more of a sight to look at. But the classical outfit in belly dancing is composed of a bra and underpants that have been enriched with tulle.

Some dancers choose to have tassels hanging down the belt, so that the hip movements can be exaggerated. Whatever she wears, the oriental dancer wears a costume which is a signal of sexuality. The costume is always attractive, seductive, arousing and revealing. And it is in accordance with the aim of the dance because sex appeal deserves that kind of an outfit. Turkish belly

Young dancer checks her costume before a performance.

Young dancer Selinay.

Young dancers before a Queen of Dancers contest.

dancers never hesitate to wear that which is true to the original purpose.

They choose big and showy jewels for the arms and legs, and sometimes wear a crown which is the coat of arms of a queen or goddess. A tambourine with cymbals or a cane can be used as accessories depending on the kind of dance the dancer will perform for her audience. The Sword Dance was common in Arab countries became transformed in time and is now performed with a cane instead.

The Princess (Banu) dances with a cane in Tunis.

111

A SHOW PROGRAM OF ORIENTAL DANCE

Turkish belly dancers go on the stage in order to show all the flexibility and talents of the female body. They clink their cymbals to the melodies they have chosen themselves and kindle a fire in the male heart. The stage performance is programmed but the general attitude of the audience and the dancer's mood determine the actual length of her stay on it. But still, a belly dancer's program lasts 30-40 minutes and if there is time to collect tips, it can go to 45 minutes.

A SHOW PROGRAM

- The dancer appears on the stage with the first notes of the oriental music. She has cymbals on her fingers and has half-covered her face and body with the tulle which she will throw

Özel Türkbaş demonstrates the hip jerk.

112

away later on.

- She starts with a 2/4 rhythm and tours the stage.

- She sticks out her right foot and jerks her right hip and then does the same with her left foot and hip.

- As she swivels her hips, she begins to lift them up. Her hips sway right and left but she jerks it suddenly upwards in between.

- She opens her legs a little and draws a circle with her hips.

- She stands at a spot and twirls around her own axis.

- She simply walks on the stage and as she does so, she begins to move her shoulders.

- She stands and shakes her hips and shoulders together.

- She shakes her hips right and left to the tempo of the percussion instrument. She can also do this in a single direction.

- The rhythm changes. She makes slow turns, tosses her hips and finishes this part.

- The drums play solo and the dancer matches the movements of her abdomen to the sound of the drum. She does

Özel Türkbaş demonstrates the turns during a dance.

Özel Türkbaş demonstrating the "greeting" figures.

this as long as the drum sounds.

- She turns around a few times at the spot where she stands and does a Turkish stand with her hands crossed over her head.

- The instruments begin to play a *Karshilama* (greeting). The rhythm is 9/8 now. She starts walking with her right foot and after 4 beats, she jumps lightly on her left foot. If she starts walking with her left foot, she jumps on her right one after 4 beats.

- She continues to walk with *Karshilama* steps and tours the stage once. Then she walks with the same steps in a more confined area.

- She starts to quiver her tummy.

- She suddenly tosses her hips one after the other.

- She roams about and as she does, she moves her shoulders, jerks them one by one, wriggling them as she goes.

- She puts her knees on the ground, opens up her legs a little and leans back so that her head touches the ground. She rocks

Özel Türkbaş drawing a circle with the hips.

her hips to the music in this position. She sways to the right and then to the left on the ground.

- She stands up slowly and begins to vibrate her hips. The vibrations here are tiny and she has her back to the audience.

- She makes turns again. She finishes her program facing the audience and bows to the applause.

- As she walks around, she swings her hips right and left abruptly.

- She twirls at the spot where she stands.

- She completes the dance with a classic Turkish stance and salutes the audience as long as the applause goes on. This is a span of time when she rests a little.

- She begins a slow turn with a 4/4 rhythm and puts off the tulle wrap around her body. She may go on dancing with the tulle in her hands.

- She walks around on the stage and takes off the veil if she has any.

- She draws an 8 where she stands using the tulle or the veil in her hand.

- She whirls the tulle and throws it onto the stage.

- She moves her arms like a snake and her hand movements resemble those of a cobra, doing one of the most accustomed motions of oriental dance.

- She stands where she is, inhaling and exhaling with her belly so that it moves in and out.

- She draws circles with her belly as she walks. She kneels on the floor inclining right and left on her knees. She sits on the floor and then rises on her feet, sticking out her neck right and left like Indian dancers. In the meantime, her hands are crossed over her head (the Turkish stance).

- She draws circles with her shoulders, swaying her hips right and left. Then she assumes a standing position.

- Then, she does the camel walk. This is done by walking around on the stage. She continues to twirl around her own axis.

Özel Türkbaş showing a back bend.

116

- She stands still and finishes the program with the cobra movement.

- The drums or the "darbuka" (rhythmic instrument in the shape of an earthenware pitcher with a skin covering the bottom) performs solo.

- She clinks the cymbals.

- She stands and jerks her hips to the right and to the left.

- She thrusts her legs to the front one after the other and jerks out the corresponding hip as she does it.

- She draws circles with her hips.

- She takes up a simple walk on the stage and leaves it walking as such.[10]

The dancer who succeeds in establishing a warm relationship with the audience usually returns to the stage once or twice to dance a little longer. If she does so, she repeats the most difficult routines which people have applauded most.

An oriental dancer walks among the tables in the accompaniment of a drum solo to collect tips. She asks for it if she pleases. She goes up to the spectators and shakes her tits. A worthy spectator thrusts the right number of bills between her breasts or into her bra. The dancer leans towards the spectator to coax him to tip her. If she is met with an enthusiastic spectator, she may even dance on the table. Famous dancers do not collect tips and refrain from doing these actions.

The single-program performance given above is not standard, but is one of which Özel Türkbaş, a very famous Turkish dancer in the USA, has proposed in her instruction course. Turkish oriental dancers devise their own programs according to their individual talents and tastes.

THE MASTERS
OF TURKISH BELLY DANCING

Large publics have appreciated the outstanding talents of some belly dancers who have danced on Turkish and world stages for many years. It would be extremely disloyal not to give the names of those dancers who were as sweet as "Turkish delight" and who have presented a dream world to their admirers every time they began to shake their hips. There would

Emine Adalet Pee, the first Turkish belly dancer on the stage.

be nothing called "Turkish Belly Dancing" without those stars who have twinkled in music halls and dancing theaters.

The most renowned belly dancer during the first years of the Turkish Republic (founded in 1923) was Emine Adalet Pee, who was born in 1909. She took to dancing at the age of 14. She married a German, hence her surname, and went to Germany to further her dance career. She danced on American, Egyptian and English stages and performed in front of statesmen such as Atatürk, King George V and Adolf Hitler. She was so famous in Germany, that they put a train wagon at her disposal when she

Two masters in the 50s: Nergis Mogol (left) and Hülya Alp (right).

Two Turkish dancers who were famous in the USA in the 70's:
Necla Ateş and Özel Türkbaş (on the opposite page).

traveled from Vienna to Berlin by rail.

Born in 1923, Nergis Mogol first appeared on stage in
Istanbul at the age of three. She was not only famous in Turkey
but also in Baghdad, Beirut, Damascus and Kuwait. She has
taught belly dancing to the following dancers: Nimet Alp,
Melike Cemali, Türkan Şamil, and Saliha Tekneci became
renowned and cherished in the 1950's. Many of them shook the
stages of the Middle East, in the Mediterranean countries and in
the U.S.

Necla Ateş became the most famous dancer in the U.S. She
has also mystified the directors in Hollywood and played in
movies. She was called "Turkish Delight" and was the biggest
master in the "fire dance." She became the first dancer in the

The mythical dancer Ayşe Nana (above and on the opposite page).

Broadway musical "Fanny" and added the eastern touch to the stages in New York.

Another Turkish belly dancer who hit the lines in the USA was Özel Türkbaş. İt is correct to say, that the American predilection for belly dancing owes a great deal to these two dancers. Many American women have learned to "make their

 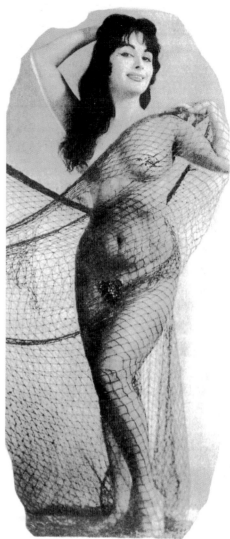

İnci Birol who shook İstanbul (left) and Semiramis who danced in many countries (right) in the 60s.

husbands sultans" in Özel Türkbaş's school and from her book on oriental dancing. Türkbaş has also produced records and casettes with eastern music and taught her students to shake their hips to those oriental melodies. Özel Türkbaş had a very dainty figure and she has danced as a representative of Turkey in many performances abroad.

Ayşe Nana was a dancer who shook Istanbul with her long black hair, harmonious body structure and voluptuous lips at

Aysel Tanju: The goddess of oriental dance in the 60s.

Actress and dancer Leyla Sayar (left), the goddess of sex appeal
Özcan Tekgül (right) and the black beauty Tahiye Salem in the 60s.

Nilüfer Aydan, anot
master in the 6

the end of the 50's. She was the one who added striptease to her dance and fluttered all the pulses. There are still hundreds of witnesses who tell about the shaking orgasms she has had on a piano every night. Ayşe Nana went to Italy afterwards and shook the European press this time with her scandals. She united belly dancing with strip-tease in Italy and danced for many years.

Semiramis, Babuş who conquered Anatolia with her plump, quivering body. İnci Birol and Semra Yıldız, the legendary dancers of not only Turkey but also the whole Middle East, were the most prominent stars in the 1960's. Another legend in the 60's was Aysel Tanju who was famed to be the most erotic dancer who danced in a trance. She was the belly dancer who made the audience rattle with passion. She was erotic even if she danced in her everyday clothes. The public called her "the goddess of sex" and she played such a character in the movies.

Özcan Tekgül was born in 1941 and was one of the most talented dancers audiences have seen. She danced like in a dream and she could stay on the stage for a long period. She made a bet in 1967 and danced on her knees for a whole 6.5 hours, breaking a world record. She also acted in movies.

The apples of the eye in the late 60's were Leyla Sayar, Birsen Ayda, Nilüfer Aydan, Tehiye Salem, Sedef Türkay, the Gülay sisters and Zennube to whom songs were dedicated[11].

The beloved dancers in the 80's were Nesrin Topkapi, Seher Şeniz and Princess Banu who all had extraordinary talents. Nesrin Topkapi was the first belly dancer to perform a show in the Turkish TV at a time when belly dancing was banned. Topkapi is one of the most beloved masters of Turkish belly dancing who succeeded to make each show a work of art. She established a school in Germany in the 90's and teaches there.

Seher Şeniz was a beautiful belly dancer. She was the last star to enrich her magical dancing with sex appeal. She, too, united her dancing with strip-tease and acted in the movies which the

Hülya Işıl, a renowned dancer in the 90s.

Nesrin Topkapı, the grand master who was the first dancer to appear on TV in the 80s.

Seher Şeniz, the beautifully erotic dancer and actress in the 80s.

public appreciated very much.

Princess Banu is one of the most famous representatives of Turkish belly dancing with her tall body and harmonious curves. She is a real star who has danced almost in all foreign countries. In her own words, she is a dancer "who lives and makes love with dance." She is also the best interpreter of the

Tülay Karaca, one of the last grand masters (left),
young dancers Leyla Adalı and Sibel Gökçe (right).

Egyptian school of dancing. She has been an astounding star on
the stages in Europe, the Middle East and North Africa. She has

Unforgettable Sibel Can (90s) who
became an actress and singer.

Asena, a beautiful, original and favored dancer today.

also danced on behalf of the Ministry of Tourism. Gamze Öz who became famous first in Holland, Hülya Işil who has a very agile body, Yonca Yücel who has been a star in Cairo and in many other Arab countries, Efruz and Tülay Karaca who has always been number one in the touristic dance halls in Istanbul are among the latest masters of Turkish oriental dancing.

Sibel Can who put an end to her dancing and became a singer; Şıvga Zinnur Karaca and Emmune Cemali who continue

Tanyeli, one of the best and most popular dancers today.

Sultana, the Queen of Turkish Belly Dancers contest in 1999.

with this family tradition, Sibel Bariş, a very talented young master, Tanyeli, a swift, attractive and young artist, and Asena, the latest popular talent are the best Turkish dancers today.

Many other dancers whom we have not added to the list here are clinking their cymbals on stage with the desire and the determination to become masters of an art they have fallen in love with.

A GUIDE TO WATCH AN ORIENTAL DANCE PERFORMANCE

Dear spectator,

As everyone knows, the talents, education and character structure of a person are the entities which determine his

Şehrazat, a famous dancer in the 50s.

conception of art. But it requires neither a higher education nor any special talent to enjoy oriental belly dancing. It involuntarily asks you to give way to your innate tendency to sensuality. In

Tülay Karaca walks on the stage   139
in " welcoming" steps.

Semra among her guests.

short, this kind of dancing is just a very delicate, feminine and voluptuous call to sexuality.

Oriental music, the curling choreography and those lively costumes are nothing but elements which are there to increase the violence in that sexual invitation.

The oriental belly dance is the rhythmical expression of the female's sacred capacity to give birth to life and of the desire to copulate. In other words, it is the free and feminine expression of the human being's innate craving to perpetuate his kind. This universal feeling makes this dance attract attention and arouse interest all around the world.

Young dancer Nergis.

Dear oriental dance spectator,

You are now face to face with a sacred call which dates back to hundreds of years, and which every society has molded according to its own tastes and ethics. This dance does not resemble the ones with strict rules which the middle classes perform in confined halls. Neither is it like the modern dances which satisfy the need for entertainment during a week-end in a disco. The oriental dancer makes you see something natural; a dance which has the reflections of the old ages when man had to strive so hard to keep himself alive in a hostile nature.

Here she is on stage; she is wearing an array which conceals

143

that beautiful feminine body just enough, provoking the passion which is already in you.

The dancer falls prey to the oriental music which conquers her inside, rejoices in it and loses control over her own feelings.

Her body becomes the instrument to reveal her emotions. Her mimics and the tremor in her body show a kind of speech which she does all by herself. The conversation between the feminine body and the feminine soul, the harmony and the discrepancy in between are explicit in the dancer's movements.

The dancer lets her body cry out its irresistible longings. She succeeds in displaying an unsurpassed dance show as long as she sincerely transforms that sensuality into her body language. And then comes the moment when she herself becomes the slave of both her body and her dance.

She reflects the feminine

Asuman Can, a dancer in the 60s.

Ayla, a young and favored dancer in the 70s.

love and desire in her person in the turns, twists and jerks of her dance. The Turkish oriental belly dancer does not only convey her sensuality, she also encourages you to feel and to react to them.

The spectator always perceives that call because he, too, has that sensuality imbedded in him. Then, the spectator becomes one with the dancer; the eros in his body begins to twitch to the music and the cymbals; his libido catches on fire. The electric current that has infiltrated the body moves down to the heart and down to the bowels. So, please submit to the dancer! Let her show you all her talents, captivate you and feel to be your master...

A tourist bewitched by the dancer.

I want to remind you of the music accompanying that dance; the violin's agility, the clarinet's naughtiness, the speed of the *cümbüş*, the poignant tone of the *kanun* and the drum's arousing tempo simply have to be there to compose that special music which has come to existence with an oriental society's taste and through years of effort. I am sure you will also be convinced, that this music is the twin of the dance.

Of course, many shows are just there to fulfil an hour on the stage and then retreat. Some dancers do their job not only professionally but also mechanically. Well, it is bad luck to be confronted with only a bread-winner and a machine instead of a full woman who fumes with voluptuousness.

A spectator dreaming of something private.

Swift-footed Şehrazat dancing in the 50s.

In a good belly dance show, the dancer and the musicians are in an uninterrupted dialogue. The dancer senses the fire in her spectators and talks with the instruments accordingly. Usually, a frivolous conversation goes on between the dancer and the music; and the drums, the clarinet, her body and the cymbals on her dainty fingers are the means of that dialogue. At such instances, the improvisations which are so natural to jazz become akin to oriental music. The musician regulates the rhythm and takes the lead, making the dancer follow the will of his heart. The dancer's body bows before the melody and the

A guest toiling to reach the goddess.

tempo, whereby it is never difficult for trained eyes to tell the difference between medium and good quality dancing.

The dancer has a subconscious too...and she wears a costume which reveals all her physical beauty. She is wrapped up in tulle which cuddles her body and her belly-long hair flies in the air as she turns. Her make up emphasizes her eyes and lips...the two most attractive parts on her face. She is beautiful. She is a queen. She is Cleopatra. She is a concubine ready to be sold at the slave market. She wears an ankle bracelet as if it were a label. Or she has a bracelet and a band around her upper arm muscle reminding us of the same deal.

The belly dancer is not a performance artist who is there to

*Princess Banu kindles
the oriental fire.*

Dancers Gülseren (left) and Aynur Ateş (right)
saluting the audience after the show.

make you enjoy a couple of hours watching the show. She is the queen who sees in you a subject in her "queendom." She wants to be desired and to feel that she is desired. She will not refrain from exhibitionism if it's necessary to feel that desire.

It is a must to appreciate her, to want her and to become her subject. She satisfies her need to own and dominate as her spectator realizes that he also becomes an owner in his own

Yeşim dancing on a table in England (1950).

Princess Banu as Cleopatra.

style. The majority of the audience will feel that it is faced with a woman who can really satisfy the god-given instincts of masculinity. Men will be happy to be men.

The dancer offers you all her beauty; she enters your eyes, heart and bowels. You are then face to face with the oriental dancer who "feels alive when she dances," who "makes love with her dance," who "feels that she's a woman only when she dances," and who even "reaches orgasm only when she dances." You are filled with those revolting instincts in you. You like to think that she is dancing for you alone. If she comes near you and calls you to join in with her clinking cymbals, she turns into a seductive goddess. Let go of yourself; let yourself be carried away to her magnetic field. Abstract yourself from what's going

Beautiful Tülay Karaca
fluttering the pulses.

Dancer Efruz.

on around you and join in the sexual ritual...

This is the magic of the oriental dance!

May God save you from resisting to this magic and ending up at a psychologist's office!

The deeper you lend an ear to the oriental music, the more chances you get to catch up with the dancer; so, let the music ooze into your body.

The oriental dancer is other women's rival. She is someone who openly calls a spouse to join in the sensual ceremony. She only uses the stage, her dress, her body and the music consciously to arouse that male spouse.

She is a teacher whom other women should carefully watch; a teacher who is at the peak of the artistic seduction. Ladies may learn how they can make their spouses feel himself to be a sultan. And you ladies, please don't be sorry! That being who mystifies men is nobody alien, it is the female herself.

The belly dancer is the most beautiful natural calamity in men's eyes; a calamity that shakes, burns and destroys...

"I rule people on the stage. When I start to dance, they fall prey to me. At that moment, I stop being an overpowered being and take zest out of overpowering myself."(12)

The dancer, who satisfies her own need to master others, acts as if she is not aware of the reflections of that sensual call.

She is a goddess who makes us wipe out our daily lives full of stress, a goddess who escorts us back to nature by triggering our most innate instincts and who invites us to the love of life. The oriental belly dance is the most powerful aphrodisiac humanity has invented in order to perpetuate itself.

What else do we have to do, dear reader, other than to enjoy this magic?

Young dancer Ayşe Yavuz.

NOTES

1. Agah Sirri Levent, Two Pamphlets Attributed to Aşik Paşa, Annual of Research on the Turkish Language, Ankara 1955, pp. 153-163.
2. Vahit Lütfi Salci, The Games of the Hidden Turkish Religion, (the first scientific research on the *sema* dances of the Bektashis and Alevis), Istanbul 1941.
3. See the works of Metin And, Mahmut R. Gazimihal and Sadi Yaver Ataman on Turkish Folk Dances. Also see, Magazine for Turkish Folklore Research.
4. Ali Riza Bey, Istanbul Once Upon A Time, pp. 298-305.
5. From Ahmet Mithat (Efendi), *Çengi*.
6. Halil Bedi Yönetken, Collection Notes İ, pp. 9-13.
7. Evliya Çelebi, The Travelbook, Ed. by Zuhuri Danişman, V.2, pp. 324-317.
8. Reşat Ekrem Koçu's works on the *köcheks*.
9. See Sadi Yaver Ataman's notes and the Magazine for Turkish Folklore Research.
10. Adapted from Özel Türkbaş, *The Belly Dancer In You*, New York 1977.
11. Ergun Hiçyilmaz, articles in *Çengis*, *Köchek*s, Transvestites, Lesbians, pp. 108-123. Also periodicals like, Gala, Paradise, The Garden of Paradise, Fairy, Sunday and Venus.
12. Akin Ok, Belly Dancers Who Seduced Istanbul.

SPECIAL THANKS TO:

The artist, Princess Banu provided me with much information on belly dancing and the psychology of the dancer. I am grateful to her.

Photographer Güngör Özsoy and the patron of second-hand book sellers in Kadiköy, Ferda Anaoğul, have told their memories to contribute to the short history of the early Republican era. May they live long with their precious memories.

I am deeply thankful to all the stars who have sent me their photographs on the stage, to photographer Mustafa Şapçi and to Foto Hikmet.

BIBLIOGRAPHY

And, Metin: Oyun Ve Büyü (Games and Spells), İş Bankasi Publications, Istanbul, 1975.

Ahmet, Mithat (Efendi): *Chengi*, Ministry of Culture Publications, Ankara, 1997.

Balikhane, Naziri Ali Riza Bey: Bir Zamanlar Istanbul (Istanbul Once Upon A Time), Tercüman 1001 Primary Works, Istanbul, (publication date is not given).

Buonaventura, Wendy: *Serpent of the Nile*, Saqi Books, London, 1974.

Evliya Çelebi: Book of Travels of Evliya Çelebi, Ed. by Zuhuri Danişman, Zuhuri Danişman Publications, Istanbul, 1969.

Hiçyilmaz, Ergun: Çengiler, Köçekler, Dönmeler, Lez'olar (*Chengi*s, *Köchek*s, Transvestites, Lesbians), Cep Books, Istanbul, 1991.

Koçu, Reşad Ekrem: Istanbul Ansiklopedisi (The Encyclopedia of Istanbul) V. İ-Xİ, Istanbul 1958-71 and his other works.

Sevengil, Refik Ahmet: Istanbul Nasil Eğleniyordu (How Istanbul Had Fun) İletişim Publications, Istanbul, 1990.

Türkbaş, Özel: *The Belly Dancer In You*, New York, 1977.

Ok, Akin: Istanbul'un Kalbini Çalan Dansözler (The Belly Dancers Who Seduced Istanbul), Broy Publications, Istanbul, 1997.

Ok, Akin: Eğlence Dünyasinin Sakli Şiddeti (The Hidden Violence of the World of Entertainment), Broy Publications, Istanbul, 1997.

Prenses Banu: Oryantal Dans Üzerine Notlar (Notes on Oriental Dancing). Unpublished notes.

Yar, Incila & Şairoğlu Hamit: Asirlar Boyu Dans ve Bale (Dance and Ballet Throughout the Ages), Istanbul, 1968.

Yönetken, Halil Bedi: Derleme Notlari (Collection Notes) I, Orkestra Publications, Istanbul, 1966.

PERIODICALS:

Peri Haftalik Magazin: Weekly magazine Peri (Fairy)
Gala Skandal Mecmuasi: Gala Scandal Magazine
Cennet Güzel Kadinlar Magazini: Cennet (Paradise)
    Magazine of Beautiful Women
Cennet Bahçesi: The Garden of Paradise
Pazar Haftalik Mecmua: Pazar (Sunday) Weekly Magazine
Venüs Haftalik Mecmua: Venüs (Venus) Weekly Magazine
Erkekçe Aylik Dergi: Erkekçe (Masculine) Monthly Magazine
Kadinca Aylik Dergi: Kadinca (Feminine) Monthly Magazine
Bravo Aylik Dergi: Bravo Monthly Magazine
Playmen Aylik Dergi: Playmen Monthly Magazine

SEXUAL LIFE
IN
OTTOMAN SOCIETY

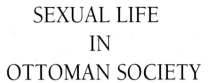

The mysterious sex life of the Ottoman society has remained a taboo until recent years. Even now it is not truly unveiled. Beyond the façade of conventional relations, the sexual life of the Ottoman society was surprisingly rich and colorful.

The Ottoman man was a conneaisseur of every kind of beauty. His addiction to all kinds of sexual experience was possible in the cosmopolitan context naturally, with a good deal of tolerance from the administrators in sexual matters.

On the other side of the coin, we find that the experiences enjoyed by the women were equally colorful. Here are some chapters from this wealth of experiences:

- The Greatest Mystery: Harem
- Professional Sex in Ottoman Society
- The Aesthetic Norms of the Ottoman Man
- Encyclopaedia of Sexology (Bahnâme)
- Çengis and Lesbiens
- Dancing Girls (Çengis) and Dancing Boys (Köçeks)
- The Domestic Mistresses: Odalisks
- Beauties of the World Through the Eyes of the Ottomans
- The Warm Nests of Love: Turkish Baths
- Homosexuality in the Ottoman Society
- Language of Flirtation
- Ottoman Sex Anecdotes
- Ottoman Texts on Sexuality
- Sex Scandals Which Shocked the Ottoman Society